A GIFT FOR:

_____

FROM:

_____

DATE:

_____

Crazy About My Sister

BARBOUR
PUBLISHING

CRAZY ABOUT MY SISTER™

COPYRIGHT © 2003 BY MARK GILROY COMMUNICATIONS, INC.
TULSA, OKLAHOMA

ART AND DESIGN BY JACKSONDESIGNCO,LLC
SILOAM SPRINGS, ARKANSAS

ISBN 1-59310-289-5

Scripture quotations marked NLT are taken from the Holy Bible, New Living
Translation, copyright © 1996. Used by permission of Tyndale House Publishers, Inc.
Wheaton, Illinois 60189, U.S.A. All rights reserved.

PUBLISHED BY BARBOUR PUBLISHING, INC., P.O. BOX 719,
UHRICHSVILLE, OHIO 44683, www.barbourpublishing.com

Member of the
Evangelical Christian
Publishers Association

PRINTED IN CHINA.

I Love You!

THERE ARE THREE THINGS
THAT WILL ENDURE ~ FAITH, HOPE,
AND LOVE ~ AND THE GREATEST
OF THESE IS LOVE.

1 CORINTHIANS 13:13 NLT

I'M CRAZY ABOUT MY SISTER
BECAUSE SHE HAS STUCK BY ME
THROUGH THICK AND THIN.

I'M CRAZY ABOUT MY SISTER
BECAUSE DAD TAUGHT US THE
IMPORTANCE OF GETTING ALONG.

I'M CRAZY ABOUT MY SISTER
BECAUSE WE'VE ALWAYS
LOOKED BEAUTIFUL TOGETHER.

I'M CRAZY ABOUT MY SISTER
BECAUSE WE'VE BOTH GROWN UP TO
BECOME SERIOUS AND MATURE WOMEN.

I'M CRAZY ABOUT MY SISTER
BECAUSE SHE AND I HAVE ALWAYS
BEEN GREAT AT SHARING.

I'M CRAZY ABOUT MY SISTER
BECAUSE WE KNOW HOW TO
MAKE EACH OTHER LAUGH.

I'M CRAZY ABOUT MY SISTER
BECAUSE WHEN WE WERE
LITTLE KIDS WE KEPT EACH OTHER
FROM GETTING SCARED AT NIGHT.

I'M CRAZY ABOUT MY SISTER
BECAUSE WE'VE ALWAYS
MADE A GREAT TEAM.

I'M CRAZY ABOUT MY SISTER
BECAUSE SHE HELPS ME STAY
UP-TO-DATE ON CURRENT EVENTS.

I'M CRAZY ABOUT MY SISTER
BECAUSE SHE AND I MAKE
BEAUTIFUL MUSIC TOGETHER.

I'M CRAZY ABOUT MY SISTER
BECAUSE OF ALL THOSE WONDERFUL
TALKS WE HAD AS LITTLE GIRLS.

I'M CRAZY ABOUT MY SISTER
BECAUSE SHE HAS A WONDERFUL
SENSE OF FAMILY VALUES.

I'M CRAZY ABOUT MY SISTER
BECAUSE WE BOTH SAVOR
LIFE'S SIMPLE PLEASURES.

I'M CRAZY ABOUT MY SISTER
BECAUSE OF OUR SHARED INTERESTS.

I'M CRAZY ABOUT MY SISTER
BECAUSE WE WERE ALWAYS
SUCH ANGELS TOGETHER.

"You girls aren't making a mess, are you?"

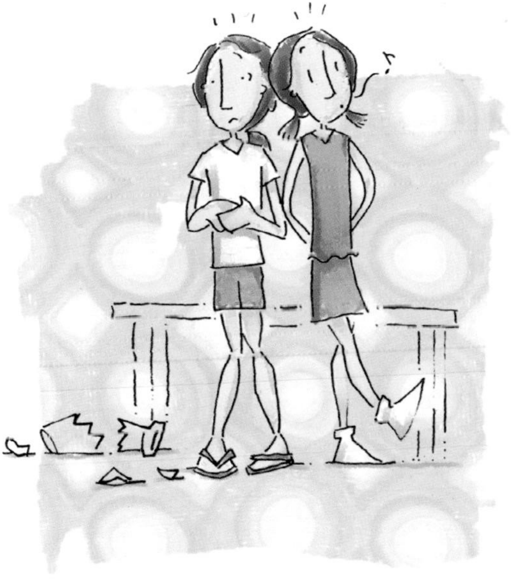

I'M CRAZY ABOUT MY SISTER
BECAUSE SHE'S SO EASY TO SHOP FOR.

I'M CRAZY ABOUT MY SISTER
BECAUSE SHE AND I ALWAYS
HAD GREAT TASTE IN MEN.

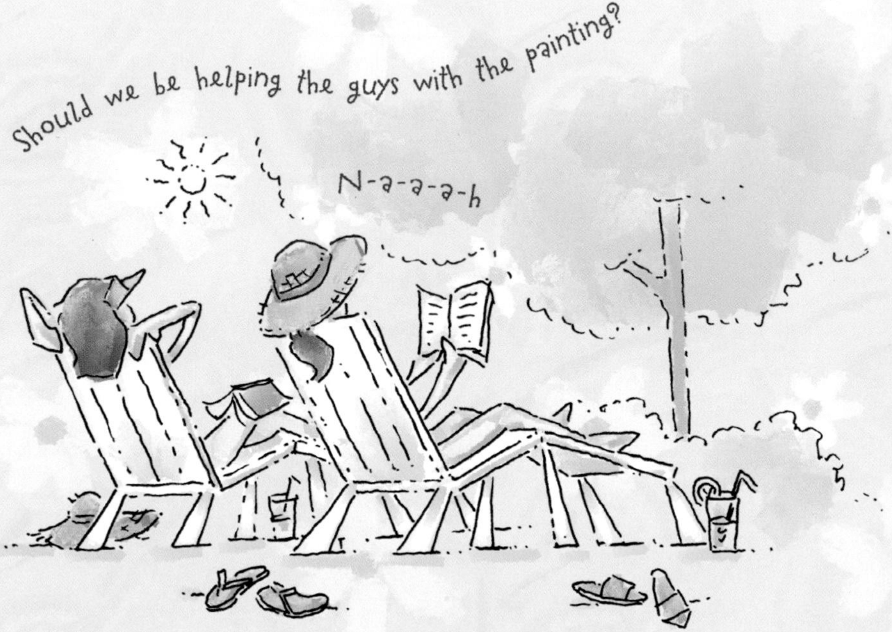
Should we be helping the guys with the painting?
N-a-a-a-h

I'M CRAZY ABOUT MY SISTER
BECAUSE SHE KNOWS THERE'S
A TIME TO SLOW DOWN
AND ENJOY GOD'S CREATION.

I'M CRAZY ABOUT MY SISTER
BECAUSE OF HER ZEST FOR LIFE!

I'M CRAZY ABOUT MY SISTER
BECAUSE SHE HAS ALWAYS BEEN
QUICK TO COME TO MY DEFENSE.

I'M CRAZY ABOUT MY SISTER
BECAUSE SHE IS THE PICTURE
OF GRACE AND POISE.

I'M CRAZY ABOUT MY SISTER
BECAUSE WE BOTH LOVE
THE HOLIDAYS.

I'M CRAZY ABOUT MY SISTER
BECAUSE SHE'S ALWAYS APPRECIATED
MY KEEN SENSE OF HUMOR.

Oh, cut it out.

I'M CRAZY ABOUT MY SISTER
BECAUSE WE AGREE ON
ALMOST EVERYTHING.

I'M CRAZY ABOUT MY SISTER
BECAUSE WE BOTH PICKED UP A
FEW "QUIRKS" FROM OUR MOTHER.

I'M CRAZY ABOUT MY SISTER
BECAUSE SHE ALWAYS
UNDERSTANDS MY MOODS.

I'M CRAZY ABOUT MY SISTER
BECAUSE SHE REALLY
CAN READ MY MIND.

Oh my...then what happened?
And then he said...let's just be friends.

I'M CRAZY ABOUT MY SISTER
BECAUSE NOTHING COULD
EVER COME BETWEEN US.

(THOUGH WE BOTH HAVE AN EYE ON MOM'S CHINA.)

I'M CRAZY ABOUT MY SISTER
BECAUSE WE'VE SURVIVED SO
MANY UPS AND DOWNS TOGETHER.

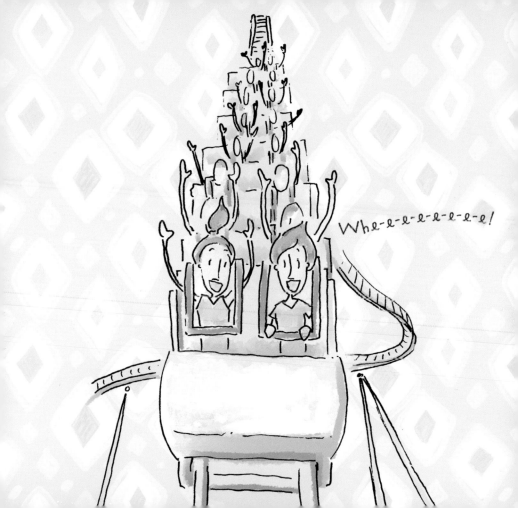

I'M CRAZY ABOUT MY SISTER
BECAUSE SHE'S COMMITTED
TO STAYING IN TOUCH WITH ME.

I'M CRAZY ABOUT MY SISTER
BECAUSE MOM ALWAYS SAID
WE WERE TWO PEAS IN A POD.

I'M CRAZY ABOUT MY SISTER
BECAUSE SHE SEES PAST MY FAULTS

(AND SHE LOVES ME ANYWAY).

I'M CRAZY ABOUT MY SISTER
BECAUSE CHILDHOOD
FAMILY VACATIONS HAVE A WAY
OF BONDING YOU FOR LIFE.

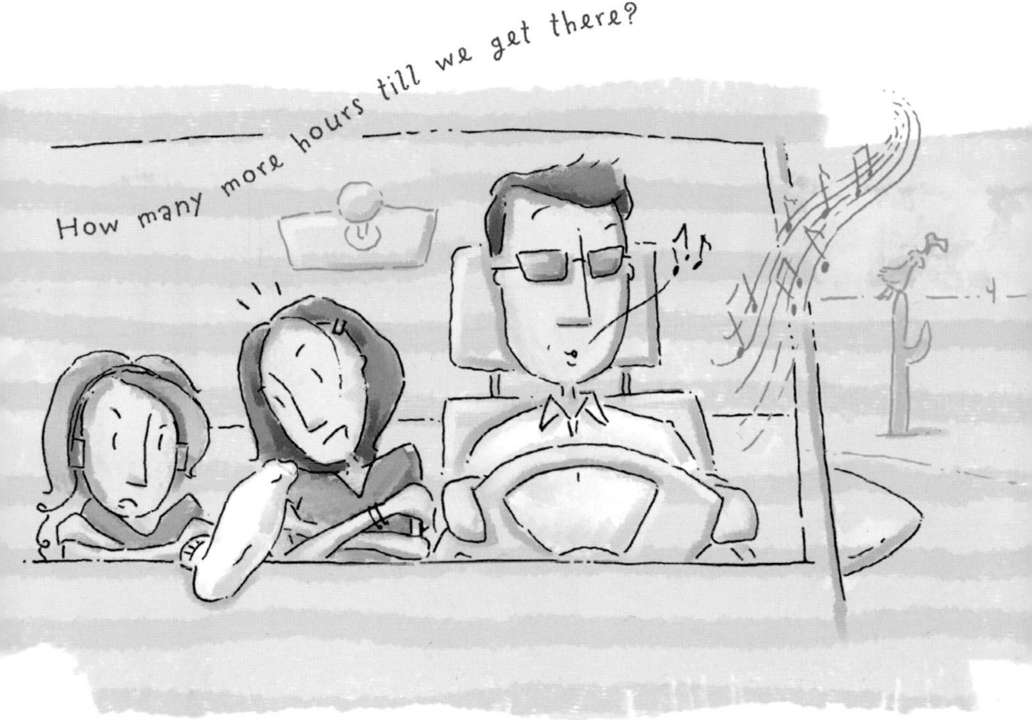
How many more hours till we get there?

I'M CRAZY ABOUT MY SISTER
BECAUSE SHE HAS ALWAYS
CHALLENGED ME TO BE MY BEST.

I'M CRAZY ABOUT MY SISTER
BECAUSE SHE HAS A BEAUTIFUL
WAY WITH WORDS AND KNOWS
HOW TO MAKE ME FEEL SPECIAL.

I'M CRAZY ABOUT MY SISTER
BECAUSE OF OUR SHARED MEMORIES
THAT WILL LAST A LIFETIME.

I'M CRAZY ABOUT MY SISTER
BECAUSE SHE LISTENS
UNTIL I'VE MANAGED TO SAY
EVERYTHING ON MY HEART.

I'M CRAZY ABOUT MY SISTER
BECAUSE SHE'S CRAZY ABOUT ME.

I'M CRAZY ABOUT MY SISTER
BECAUSE I'M POSITIVE THAT GOD SENT
HER AS AN ANGEL TO BLESS MY LIFE.

I'M CRAZY ABOUT MY SISTER
BECAUSE THERE'S NO OTHER
EXPLANATION FOR WHY I MISS HER
SO MUCH WHEN WE'RE NOT TOGETHER.

I'M CRAZY ABOUT MY SISTER
BECAUSE SHE HAS
A FORGIVING SPIRIT.

I'M CRAZY ABOUT MY SISTER
BECAUSE WE BOTH LOVE
THE SAME WONDERFUL FATHER.

I'M CRAZY ABOUT MY SISTER
BECAUSE SHE HAS ALWAYS KNOWN
EXACTLY THE RIGHT THING TO SAY
WHEN I NEED CHEERING UP.

I'M CRAZY ABOUT MY SISTER
BECAUSE I NEED SOMEONE WHO
LOVES ME ENOUGH TO PRAY FOR ME.

(I PRAY FOR HER, TOO.)

I'M CRAZY ABOUT MY SISTER
BECAUSE EVEN WHEN WE
GET OLD AND WRINKLED—
WE WILL STILL BE ROCKING!